Álvaro Fonseca
Davis Brenes
Carlos Mendoza

# The Digital Era in Production

Álvaro Fonseca
Davis Brenes
Carlos Mendoza

# The Digital Era in Production

## Strategies for Industry 4.0

ScienciaScripts

**Imprint**
Any brand names and product names mentioned in this book are subject to trademark, brand or patent protection and are trademarks or registered trademarks of their respective holders. The use of brand names, product names, common names, trade names, product descriptions etc. even without a particular marking in this work is in no way to be construed to mean that such names may be regarded as unrestricted in respect of trademark and brand protection legislation and could thus be used by anyone.

Cover image: www.ingimage.com

This book is a translation from the original published under ISBN 978-613-9-46929-1.

Publisher:
Sciencia Scripts
is a trademark of
Dodo Books Indian Ocean Ltd. and OmniScriptum S.R.L publishing group

120 High Road, East Finchley, London, N2 9ED, United Kingdom
Str. Armeneasca 28/1, office 1, Chisinau MD-2012, Republic of Moldova, Europe
Managing Directors: Ieva Konstantinova, Victoria Ursu
info@omniscriptum.com

Printed at: see last page
**ISBN: 978-620-8-39771-5**

# Table of Contents

## For the Reader

In this book, we invite you on a fascinating journey through the heart of the Digital Age and its transformative impact on Industry 4.0. This journey goes beyond the technical; it is designed to show you, in a clear and accessible way, how technology is revolutionizing production at all levels. Here, you will understand how tools such as artificial intelligence, the Internet of Things (IoT), and automation are changing not only the way we work, but also the way we conceive of production itself. We want you to feel this advancement not as an intimidating challenge, but as an exciting opportunity to evolve and reach new possibilities in the world of work.

The structure of the book will guide you step by step. We start with the basic concepts to cement a solid understanding of what Industry 4.0 means and how it differs from previous industrial models. In this first part, you will discover the foundations that will allow you to understand the paradigm shift we are living through. As you progress, each chapter delves into specific strategies and practical applications, providing examples and case studies that will help you visualize how these concepts apply in the real world. Here you will not only see theory; each page seeks to give you the necessary tools to imagine and apply this knowledge in different productive contexts. At the end of the tour, you will find a reflection on the future of the industry and an invitation to actively participate in this transformation, integrating what you have learned here into your professional life.

This book is not only intended to inform you; it is also designed to inspire, motivate and encourage you to join the digital evolution that surrounds us. On each page, we have included reflections that will help you understand not only the "how" of digitalization, but also the "why". Because behind every advance, there are people like you and me who make this transformation possible. We want you to feel that you are part of something bigger and that your skills and knowledge can make a significant difference in this new environment. Get ready to dive into the fascinating world of innovation and technology, and remember that this evolution is at your fingertips. Welcome to this adventure in the Digital Age!

# Introduction

Digital transformation has revolutionized the way industries operate, and the advent of Industry 4.0 marks a significant milestone in this process. This book explores in depth the concepts, technologies, challenges and opportunities that define this new industrial era. As technology advances, the integration of physical and digital systems becomes an imperative for companies seeking to remain competitive in a rapidly changing global environment.

Industry 4.0 is not just about automating processes; it involves a profound reconfiguration of the way organizations think about production, supply chain and customer interaction. Technologies such as the Internet of Things (IoT), artificial intelligence (AI), data analytics and robotics are changing not only how goods and services are produced, but also how they are managed and distributed.

This book is structured in several chapters that address different aspects of Industry 4.0. We begin with an introduction to the fundamental concepts and key technologies that underpin it, followed by an analysis of the impact these innovations have on sustainability and operational efficiency. We also discuss the challenges companies face in implementing these technologies, including cybersecurity, resistance to change, and the upfront investment required for transformation.

In addition, future trends that will shape Industry 4.0, such as advanced artificial intelligence and digital twins, are examined, and the crucial role of education and training in preparing a workforce that can thrive in this new environment is discussed.

In conclusion, this book seeks to provide a comprehensive guide to understanding and navigating the complex landscape of Industry 4.0. Through case studies, trend analysis, and references to current literature, readers will gain an in-depth understanding of how digital transformation is redefining the future of production and business, and how they can actively participate in this evolution. Industry 4.0 is not just a passing trend; it is a paradigm shift that offers both challenges and opportunities, and is essential for any organization aspiring to succeed in the 21st century.

# Chapter 1: Introduction to Industry 4.0

Industry 4.0 represents the fourth industrial revolution, characterized by the integration of digital and physical technologies into production processes and business models globally. This chapter provides an overview of the key concepts, underlying technologies, their impact on sustainability, implementation challenges and future prospects for the industry.

## Definition and Key Concepts

Industry 4.0 refers to a new production paradigm that integrates advanced technologies such as the Internet of Things (IoT), artificial intelligence (AI), robotics, and Big Data into industrial processes. This approach promotes process automation, system interconnection, and real-time responsiveness, allowing companies to quickly adapt to market changes and improve operational efficiency. In this context, product and service customization becomes more accessible, which in turn enhances the customer experience. The concept encompasses not only production, but also design, logistics, supply chain and product lifecycle management.

## Industry 4.0 Key Technologies

Industry 4.0 key technologies refer to the set of advanced technologies that are driving the transformation of manufacturing and other industrial sectors in the Fourth Industrial Revolution. These technologies, which include the Internet of Things (IoT), big data and data analytics, artificial intelligence (AI), cyber-physical systems (CFS), robotics, additive manufacturing (3D printing), augmented reality (AR), virtual reality (VR) and cloud computing, are reshaping traditional production processes, improving efficiency and enabling smarter data-driven decision making. Their integration fosters a paradigm shift in manufacturing, facilitating the emergence of smart factories and autonomous production systems that respond dynamically to market demands and operational challenges.

The importance of these technologies lies in their ability to create interconnected environments where machines, systems and people work collaboratively to improve productivity and innovation. For example, IoT enables real-time data collection and analysis, which, combined with Big Data and AI, improves predictive maintenance and operational optimization.

Robotics and automation are increasingly used to manage complex tasks and improve safety, while additive manufacturing promotes customization and waste reduction in production processes. However, the widespread adoption of these technologies also poses challenges, such as cybersecurity concerns, the need for standardization, and potential job displacement due to automation.

Controversies surrounding key Industry 4.0 technologies often center on the implications of automation for employment and the ethical considerations of data privacy and security. Critics argue that increased reliance on AI and robotics may lead to significant job losses, particularly in low-skilled sectors, while proponents claim that these technologies will create new job opportunities and improve the overall quality of work.

In addition, concerns about data breaches and the ethical use of AI are driving discussions about the need for regulatory frameworks to ensure the responsible deployment of these technologies in industrial settings.

As industries continue to navigate the complexities of digital transformation, the integration of key Industry 4.0 technologies is essential to maintain competitiveness and foster sustainable growth. Ongoing research and development in these areas promise to further enhance operational capabilities and drive innovation in various sectors, paving the way for a more interconnected and efficient industrial landscape.

***Internet of Things (IoT)***

The Internet of Things (IoT) is a transformative network of interconnected physical devices that are equipped with sensors, software and connectivity features, enabling them to collect and exchange data over the Internet or private networks. Introduced by Kevin Ashton in 1999, the concept has significantly evolved and gained traction across diverse industries, influencing how we live and work today.

The Internet of Things (IoT) encompasses a wide range of applications, including smart homes, healthcare monitoring, industrial automation and transportation systems. Its ability to create an integrated and interconnected environment facilitates automation, optimization and real-time monitoring, improving decision-making and user experiences in the digital age.

The growing importance of IoT is evident in its integration into Industry 4.0, where it acts as a crucial enabler for greater automation and efficiency in manufacturing processes.

### *Industrial Internet of Things (IIoT)*

While IoT is often associated with consumer devices, the Industrial Internet of Things (IIoT) focuses on connected technologies within industrial environments. The IIoT uses sensors and smart machines to optimize operations, predict equipment failures and improve asset tracking in factories and warehouses. This application of IoT not only improves productivity, but also drives innovation by enabling human-robot collaboration (cobotics) and automated processes.

### *Manufacturing applications*

The Internet of Things (IoT) is revolutionizing the manufacturing industry by enabling smart factories that leverage advanced technologies such as artificial intelligence (AI), machine learning (ML) and cloud computing. These technologies facilitate real-time data analytics and predictive maintenance, helping manufacturers optimize production, improve quality control and reduce downtime.

Fortune Business Insights estimates that the IoT market in manufacturing was valued at USD 27.8 billion in 2018 and is projected to reach USD 452.27 billion by 2032, demonstrating a compound annual growth rate (CAGR) of 22.1%.

## Challenges and future directions

Despite the potential benefits, the IoT landscape faces challenges, particularly in terms of universal standardization. The lack of common standards can lead to a fragmented market, making it difficult for manufacturers to select appropriate IoT solutions and ensure interoperability between devices.

Future research is crucial to address these barriers, explore enablers, and develop strategies that leverage IoT for continued innovation and efficiency within the manufacturing sector.

As the IoT ecosystem continues to evolve, its integration with emerging technologies promises to unlock more transformative applications and benefits across diverse industries.

***Big Data and analytics***

Big Data plays a critical role in the Industry 4.0 arena, as it encompasses vast and complex data sets that traditional methods struggle to manage effectively. The ability to process and analyze these immense amounts of data generates valuable information that significantly improves manufacturing processes and decision making. Leveraging advanced computing capabilities, companies can transform raw data into actionable intelligence, which is crucial for optimizing operations and maintaining competitive advantage.

The integration of Big Data into Industry 4.0 technologies facilitates optimized processes aimed at improving manufacturing efficiency and customer service. For example, data generated from various sources, including Internet of Things sensors on factory floors, sales data and environmental factors, can be analyzed to improve production quality and logistics agility.

In addition, real-time data analysis allows manufacturers to ensure operational continuity, as any downtime can generate substantial costs.

Managing Big Data involves several challenges, particularly pending the sheer volume and complexity of data. Organizations must implement robust data storage, management and analysis tools to handle these data sets effectively. This includes using cloud computing for scalable solutions while navigating the unpredictable external environment that characterizes modern manufacturing.

Cybersecurity also becomes a critical concern, as smart interconnected systems increase vulnerability to data breaches and operational threats, requiring rigorous security measures.

### *Integration with Big Data*

The effectiveness of AI and ML in manufacturing is further enhanced with the integration of Big Data analytics. This integration enables manufacturers to create a comprehensive visualization of their operations, allowing them to identify bottlenecks, predict demand and implement strategic maintenance plans.

The synergy between AI and Big Data enables manufacturers to make informed decisions, leading to significant gains in efficiency and productivity.

### *Challenges and considerations*

Despite the potential benefits, the implementation of AI and ML in manufacturing faces challenges, primarily related to data quality and integration. Research indicates that many manufacturers struggle with inadequate data quality and poor data governance, making it difficult to develop effective AI use cases.

Ensuring that production assets generate reliable and usable data is critical to the successful implementation of AI technologies in manufacturing environments.

***Robotics and automation***

Robotics has become a fundamental element in the implementation of Industry 4.0 technology, marking a new era of smart manufacturing where robots collaborate with digital technologies such as artificial intelligence (AI) and the Internet of Things (IoT) to improve productivity and efficiency in manufacturing processes.

Robotics integration not only automates complex and repetitive tasks but also facilitates a paradigm shift towards a more sustainable and profitable economy.

**Types of robotics in manufacturing**

***Industrial robots***

Industrial robots are the most commonly used type of robots in manufacturing environments. They are characterized by their high precision and their ability to operate continuously without interruption. Typical applications include tasks such as welding, painting and assembly.

These robots significantly improve speed and accuracy, contributing to improved operational efficiency.

***Collaborative Robots***

Collaborative robots are designed to work alongside human operators, improving safety and efficiency in workflows. Equipped with advanced sensors the robots can detect the presence of humans and adapt their movements accordingly, making them suitable for tasks that require interaction with human workers, such as in packaging and material handling.

***Mobile robots***

The mobile robots navigate, independently navigate, build floors or warehouses, using sensors and cameras for obstacle avoidance. They are particularly effective for material handling, transportation and inventory. Mobile robots are seen as a potential replacement for traditional systems such as fixed conveyor belts and conventional automated guided vehicles (AGVs) in logistics.

Predictions indicate that by 2025, autonomous logistics robots will surpass the use of conventional AGVs in manufacturing environments.

***Advanced automation capabilities***

Automation is evolving to incorporate more sophisticated technologies, such as cognitive automation and data-driven decision making. Robots are increasingly integrated with AI and machine learning to perform complex tasks autonomously, leading to greater efficiency in logistics and manufacturing processes. For example, robots can autonomously perform picking, packing and quality inspection tasks, thus optimizing the entire production workflow.

In addition, the use of digital twin technology allows for virtual testing and optimization of robotic systems prior to deployment in real-world applications.

**Impact of Industry 4.0 on Sustainability**

The impact of Industry 4.0 on sustainability refers to the significant transformation in industrial and manufacturing practices driven by the integration of advanced technologies aimed at improving productivity, efficiency and environmental responsibility. Characterized by the interconnection of physical, digital and biological systems, this new era of industrial development promotes the emergence of smart factories and innovative business models that capitalize on real-time data, automation and resource management capabilities. As global industries increasingly adopt these technologies, their influence on sustainability has become a fundamental focus for researchers, policy makers and businesses alike.

The remarkable importance of Industry 4.0 lies in its dual potential to optimize production processes while addressing pressing environmental concerns. Technologies such as Internet of Things (IoT), Artificial Intelligence (AI) and advanced analytics facilitate improved energy efficiency, resource management and waste reduction, positioning companies to contribute affirmatively to environmental sustainability goals. For instance, smart manufacturing practices have been shown to reduce energy consumption by up to 30% in specific applications, underscoring the environmental benefit of digital transformation in industrial environments.

However, the integration of Industry 4.0 technologies is not without its challenges and controversies. Initial implementation costs, the need to retrain the workforce, and concerns about increased energy consumption in certain contexts have sparked debates about the overall net impact of these advances on sustainability. Critics argue that while digitization of manufacturing can lead to efficiencies, it can also exacerbate energy demands and complicate resource management if not carefully regulated.

In summary, the impact of Industry 4.0 on sustainability encapsulates both transformative opportunities and critical challenges. As industries navigate this technological shift, the imperative for sustainable practices will be central to realizing the full benefits of advanced manufacturing while mitigating potential adverse effects on the environment and society.

### *Environmental Impact*

The integration of Industry 4.0 technologies is poised to significantly influence environmental sustainability through improved energy efficiency and resource management. The operational demand for Industry 4.0 requires dynamically configurable production processes that are expected to increase primary energy consumption in manufacturing environments.

However, this digitization also offers opportunities for energy savings, with reports indicating that optimization software tools can reduce energy consumption. consumption by up to 30 % in industrial robotics applications.

The potential for energy optimization is further supported by smart energy allocation strategies that use big data analytics to improve overall energy management across manufacturing systems.

### *Economic impact*

The economic impact of Industry 4.0 is multifaceted and encompasses several dimensions that influence efficiency, cost savings and overall business performance. One of the main economic benefits of Industry 4.0 is the potential for significant savings through more accurate planning and shorter lead times, which improve energy efficiency and reduce operating costs.

By integrating advanced technologies such as the Industrial Internet of Things (IIoT) and computer simulation modeling, companies can better estimate financial benefits and economic effectiveness, which traditionally posed challenges due to their costly nature.

***Cost efficiency and resource management***

Industry 4.0 technologies contribute to improved resource management and profitability. Digitization and automation of processes enable real-time monitoring and control, resulting in reduced manufacturing waste and improved energy consumption patterns.

For example, the implementation of smart manufacturing solutions can lead to a substantial reduction in waste; studies indicate that material waste can be reduced by up to 25% after the adoption of specific technologies.

***Revenue growth and new business models***

The integration of digital and physical technologies also opens avenues for revenue growth by creating new business outcomes. Companies can develop disruptive business models, such as selling product functionality rather than simply the tangible product, which can improve customer satisfaction and loyalty while promoting sustainability.

This change not only generates new sources of revenue, but also aligns with sustainability initiatives by encouraging eco-innovation and the use of lighter, more sustainable materials in product design.

***Long-term economic considerations***

From a long-term perspective, the adoption of Industry 4.0 technologies requires a reassessment of workforce dynamics. As automation increases, companies face challenges related to job displacement and the need to upgrade the skills of existing employees.

Managers recognize the importance of training programs to equip the workforce with the skills needed to adapt to new technologies and remain competitive in a rapidly changing marketplace.

This focus on skill development is critical to fostering a sustainable business environment that balances economic growth with social responsibility.

**Social impact**

The advent of Industry 4.0 is transforming not only economic paradigms, but also social structures and the dynamic workforce. This change encompasses several elements, including improved worker safety, job satisfaction and social welfare, leading toward a more inclusive and equitable working environment.

***Worker safety and training***

Technologies such as Augmented Reality (AR) and Mixed Reality (MR) have significantly improved worker training efficiency and safety protocols. By providing real-time guidance during tasks, these technologies help reduce errors and increase the quality of manufactured products, thereby fostering a safer workplace environment.

The integration of these technologies has also contributed towards social sustainability by minimizing workplace hazards and improving the overall training experience for employees.

***Employee Commitment and development***

Employee engagement is critical to successful transformations associated with Industry 4.0. Organizations that prioritize employee participation in the decision-making process tend to achieve better results during their digital transformation initiatives. This involvement is facilitated through initiatives that promote learning and development, empowering employees to acquire new skills needed to adapt to technological changes.

For example, companies are focusing on job-specific skills development, which is crucial to improving living standards and increasing per capita income in the workforce.

***Economic and social well-being***

The social impact of Industry 4.0 extends to broader economic improvements, particularly in developing countries. The emphasis on creating smart, sustainable factories and business networks supports practices that can alleviate extreme poverty and promote dignity and equality within a healthy environment.

With the potential for significant advances in corporate social responsibility,

Industry 4.0 initiatives can lead to better working conditions and improved job satisfaction, thereby improving the overall quality of life for workers.

### *Challenges and considerations*

Despite the positive social impacts, there are challenges that need to be addressed. The shift towards more automated processes may result in job losses in certain sectors, making robust retraining programs necessary to prepare the workforce for new roles within the changing industrial landscape.

In addition, the balance between hiring new talent and training existing employees varies by region, and there are different perspectives on the best approach to workforce transformation.

The implementation of Industry 4.0 technologies presents numerous challenges and risks that can affect environmental sustainability. As organizations integrate smart and connected technologies into their manufacturing processes, they face inherent environmental challenges that require constant monitoring and adaptation of production processes to meet new energy consumption and resource management demands.

### *Environmental challenges*

The transition to Industry 4.0 often involves substantial investments in new machinery, sensors and advanced computer systems. Changes can lead to increased primary energy consumption, which carries risks to environmental sustainability if not managed effectively.

The integration of Cyber Physical Systems (CPS) demands not only financial resources, but also a significant commitment to infrastructure development, which can strain both natural and man-made resources.

In addition, while digitization offers opportunities for energy savings through optimization software and IoT integration, the potential increase in material usage and operational complexity could undermine these benefits, leading to negative environmental impacts.

The tension between the promise of energy efficiency and the reality of increased energy demands reflects the dual nature of these technological advances.

***Scenario-based analysis***

To better understand the long-term impacts of Industry 4.0, a scenario-based approach has been employed to identify several potential futures depending on the different fulfillment of the Sustainable Development Goals (SDGs).

These scenarios illustrate how factors such as technology adaptation and resource allocation can create divergent paths to sustainability. For example, while some scenarios predict a positive impact on sustainability during the operational phases, others suggest negative outcomes during the implementation stage due to the large resource demands of initial deployment.

***Social implications***

The social dimension of Industry 4.0 also presents challenges. Workforce engagement is critical to a successful transformation; without it, companies may struggle to scale their initiatives.

Employees must not only adapt to new technologies, but also contribute to a culture of sustainability within the organization. perception that job security can be compromised and can lead to resistance among workers, further complicating the implementation process.

Therefore, addressing the human element: ensuring that technological advances align with the values and needs of employees - is central to achieving sustainable results in Industry 4.0. Organizations should prioritize the creation of meaningful workplaces that not only focus on technological transformation, but also improve the well-being of their workforce, thereby fostering a more sustainable operational environment.

## Case studies

### *Overview of Industry 4.0 implementations.*

Industry 4.0 technologies have been applied in a variety of manufacturing environments to improve sustainability through increased efficiency and reduced environmental impact. These implementations serve as key case studies to illustrate the practical benefits and challenges associated with adopting advanced manufacturing practices.

### *Infineon's smart factory*

Located in Dresden, Germany, Infineon's elegant showcase factory is one of the most intelligent manufacturing networks worldwide. This facility specializes in semiconductor production and employs over 200 robots to assist in production, thereby improving manufacturing efficiency and accuracy.

All factory systems are interconnected through an advanced IT infrastructure, enabling real-time communication and data management. This integration facilitates better resource management and minimizes energy consumption, further contributing to sustainable manufacturing practices.

***Haier Group***

The Haier Group in Qingdao, China, is another outstanding example of how Industry 4.0 technologies improve sustainability. The company uses a decentralized manufacturing approach that empowers local units to make independent decisions, optimizing production based on demand in real time.

***Adidas Speed Factory***

The Adidas Speed Factory in Ansbach, Germany, represents a shift toward greater sustainability. production through the use of advanced manufacturing technologies. By adopting a model manufacturing network, Adidas has been able to reduce lead times and improve product customization while minimizing environmental impacts associated with mass production.

The integration of digital tools allows Adidas to respond quickly to market changes, leading to more responsible consumption patterns.

***Johnson & Johnson DePuy Synthesis***

In Ireland, Johnson & Johnson's DePuy Synthes division has implemented

Industry 4.0 technologies to optimize operations and improve product quality. Real-time data analytics application allows the company to monitor production processes closely, reducing the likelihood of defects and waste.

This focus on quality and efficiency not only supports sustainability, but also improves overall competitiveness in the healthcare sector.

**Future of Industry 4.0**

The future of Industry 4.0 represents a transformative change in industrial and manufacturing practices, characterized by the integration of advanced digital technologies such as artificial intelligence (AI), the Internet of Things (IoT) and robotics into traditional production processes. This Fourth Industrial Revolution aims to create smarter, more efficient and interconnected manufacturing systems, fundamentally altering how goods are produced and delivered across multiple sectors. As organizations adapt to these innovations, the significance for operational efficiency, sustainability and workforce needs are profound, making this topic prominent in discussions about The Future of Work and the Growing Economy. Industry 4.0 encompasses several key components, including data analytics, automation and decentralized decision making, all of which contribute to improved productivity and resource optimization. By leveraging real-time data and machine learning, manufacturers can achieve greater flexibility and responsiveness to market demands while improving quality control and reducing waste. The integration of these technologies is expected to redefine traditional manufacturing paradigms, paving the way for smart factories and reshaping supply chains globally. In addition, sustainability initiatives are increasingly becoming an integral part of Industry 4.0, with companies looking to reduce their environmental impact through eco-efficient practices enabled by digital technologies. However, the transition to Industry 4.0 is not without its challenges and controversies. Concerns about job displacement due to automation and the need to reskill workers have emerged as major issues in the discourse around this industrial revolution. In addition, companies face obstacles related to technology implementation, cybersecurity risks, and the absence of standardized regulations that could facilitate a smoother integration of new systems. These factors underscore the complexity of adopting Industry 4.0 technologies and highlight the need for strategic planning and stakeholder engagement in this rapidly evolving landscape. As Industry 4.0 continues to advance, companies face obstacles related to technology implementation, cybersecurity risks, and the absence of standardized regulations that could facilitate smoother integration of new systems. These factors underscore the complexity of adopting Industry 4.0 technologies and highlight the need for strategic planning and stakeholder engagement in this rapidly evolving landscape, develop, its significance for employment, environmental sustainability and economic resilience will be critical areas of focus. The future promises a range of new job opportunities along with the emergence of advanced manufacturing roles, emphasizing the importance of continuous learning and adaptation. In short, the future of Industry 4.0 is poised to reshape not only the manufacturing sector, but also the broader economy, creating pathways for innovation and growth that will define the industrial landscape for years to come.

### *Historical Context*

The evolution of industrial practices has undergone significant transformations, particularly during the Industrial Revolution, which is commonly segmented into two distinct phases: the First and Second Industrial Revolutions. The First Industrial Revolution, which began in Great Britain around 1760, marked a substantial shift from manual production methods to machine-based manufacturing processes, leading to significant increases in production and efficiency across various industries, especially textiles.

This period marks the introduction of critical innovations such as the steam engine and new chemical manufacturing techniques that facilitated the elevation of motorized factory systems and heralded a new era of economic growth and urbanization.

Historian Eric Hobsbawm points out that these industrial changes released unprecedented productive capacities within human societies, thus laying the groundwork for rapid economic expansion that has characterized modern economies.

As industries became mechanized, there was a profound transformation of social structures, moving populations from rural agrarian lifestyles to urban centers where factories became the new centers of employment and social life.

The Second Industrial Revolution occurred in the late 19th and early 20th centuries, marked by new technological advances, such as the emergence of electricity and the internal combustion engine. This phase introduced concepts of mass production and assembly lines, revolutionizing manufacturing processes and fostering economic interdependencies that would shape global markets.

The introduction of sophisticated manufacturing techniques and innovative business models during this time laid the foundation for today's discourse around Industry 4.0, which builds on these historic developments by integrating digital technologies and intelligent systems into production processes.

The context of these industrial revolutions is essential to understanding the ongoing transformation known as Industry 4.0, where data analytics, robotics and artificial intelligence are poised to redefine manufacturing once again, creating a landscape of smart factories and autonomous systems.

**Emphasis on Sustainability**

Sustainability is becoming an increasingly central issue in Industry 4.0, where companies face complex challenges related to carbon emissions, resource scarcity and changing consumer expectations. To address these issues, organizations are integrating digital technologies into their value chains, enhancing their sustainability efforts. This holistic approach recognizes that sustainability must be a fundamental element of production systems, not an afterthought. Companies are expected to leverage Industry 4.0 technologies to improve their environmental impact while achieving operational efficiencies and improving product quality.

**Technological advances**

The future of manufacturing is closely linked to the continued advancement of technologies such as artificial intelligence, the Internet of Things (IoT) and robotics. These innovations are transforming traditional manufacturing processes by enabling greater flexibility, productivity and quality. As these technologies converge, they are expected to create more sophisticated production systems capable of adapting to rapidly changing market demands. The integration of these technologies will enable manufacturers to achieve greater operational efficiencies and address emerging challenges more effectively.

### Data-driven decision making

The reliance on data is expected to intensify, with companies increasingly turning to advanced analytics and machine learning to improve decision-making processes. Traditional demand forecasting methods are becoming obsolete in the face of unprecedented external shocks, such as the COVID-19 pandemic, prompting companies to adopt more robust and adaptive forecasting techniques. The ability to leverage real-time data and predictive analytics will be crucial for organizations striving to maintain competitive advantages in the rapidly evolving Industry 4.0 landscape.

### Job creation and career opportunities

As Industry 4.0 advances, new job categories and career opportunities are emerging in a variety of sectors. Positions in data science, cybersecurity and advanced manufacturing are expected to be in high demand, reflecting the need for skilled professionals who can navigate this new technological terrain. Emphasizing continuous learning and skills development will be vital for individuals looking to thrive in this transformed job market.

The convergence of traditional industrial practices with advanced digital technologies is expected not only to improve productivity, but also to create a plethora of career paths that did not exist before.

# Chapter 2: Effects of Industry 4.0 on Operations of the Supply Chain.

Industry 4.0 has significantly transformed supply chain operations by integrating advanced technologies such as the Internet of Things (IoT), big data analytics and artificial intelligence (AI) into traditional manufacturing and logistics processes. This integration creates a smart manufacturing environment where real-time data and automation improve decision making and operational efficiency.

### Improved Transparency and Tracking

One of the most notable effects of Industry 4.0 on supply chain operations is improved end-to-end transparency and real-time asset tracking. The ability to monitor the entire supply chain in real time allows companies to identify the exact location of goods, whether they are on order, in transit or stored in a warehouse. This visibility not only minimizes out-of-stock situations, but also improves order accuracy and estimated time of arrival (ETAs) (Waller & Fawcett, 2013).

Transparency in the supply chain is achieved through the implementation of IoT technologies, which enable data collection through sensors and connected devices. These technologies are essential for real-time tracking, as they facilitate continuous communication between the different actors in the chain. For example, the use of RFID (Radio Frequency Identification) and barcodes enables efficient and accurate tracking of products, providing valuable information that can be used to make informed decisions (Kumar & Singh, 2019).

Improved supply chain visibility also enables companies to react quickly to disruptions. When a problem occurs, such as a transportation delay or production failure, the ability to identify the root cause immediately is crucial. This allows companies to implement quick and effective solutions, minimizing the impact on the overall operation (Waller & Fawcett, 2013).

In addition, transparency in the supply chain fosters more effective collaboration among the various stakeholders. By sharing information in real time, suppliers, manufacturers and distributors can work together more cohesively, resulting in more effective planning and agile response to market demands. This is especially important in a rapidly changing business environment, where the ability to adapt to new conditions is vital to success (Chae, 2019).

Improved asset tracking also has a positive impact on inventory management. The ability to track products and materials in real time helps companies optimize their inventory levels, reducing the need to hold large amounts of stock. This not only frees up capital that can be used in other areas of the business, but also reduces the costs associated with warehousing and inventory management (Kamble et al., 2020).

In terms of sustainability, supply chain transparency also plays a crucial role. By having better control over assets and processes, companies can identify areas where they can reduce waste and improve energy efficiency. This contributes to greater operational sustainability, aligning with consumer expectations and increasingly stringent environmental regulations (Bai et al., 2019).

Finally, implementing advanced technologies to improve transparency and tracking is not without its challenges. Companies must address issues of interoperability between systems and data security to ensure that shared information is accurate and secure. Staff training and change management are also critical aspects that must be considered to ensure a successful transition to a more digitized supply chain (Kamble et al., 2020).

### Sustainability and Eco-Efficiency

Industry 4.0 plays a crucial role in promoting sustainability in supply chains. As companies adopt digital technologies, they can implement eco-efficiency practices that positively impact various performance indicators, including cost, quality and resource management. This approach not only helps organizations reduce their ecological footprint, but also offers opportunities for innovation and continuous improvement in their operational processes.

#### *Eco-Efficiency and Waste Reduction*

Eco-efficiency refers to the creation of more goods and services using fewer resources and generating less waste and pollution. By integrating advanced technologies such as the Internet of Things (IoT) and data analytics, companies can monitor and optimize their resource consumption in real time. This allows them to identify and eliminate inefficient processes that produce waste, contributing to a more sustainable operation (Bai et al., 2019).

For example, smart factories use sensors to monitor energy and water use, allowing managers to adjust production processes to minimize consumption. According to a study by Kusiak (2018), implementing these technologies can reduce energy consumption by 20-30% and water use by 1520%, resulting in significant savings and a smaller environmental footprint.

### *Contribution to the Circular Economy*

Industry 4.0 also facilitates the transition to a circular economy, where resources are reused and recycled rather than discarded. By employing digital technologies, companies can track the life cycle of their products, enabling them to identify opportunities to reuse materials and components. This not only reduces the need for virgin resources, but also reduces the amount of waste generated (Geissdoerfer et al., 2018).

One example of this is the use of digital platforms that connect companies with recycling suppliers, allowing discarded materials to be reintroduced into the production process. This practice not only contributes to environmental sustainability, but can also result in operating cost reductions by reducing reliance on new materials.

### *Data Analysis for Sustainability*

The implementation of data analytics technologies enables companies to more accurately track their environmental performance. By analyzing data on energy, water and emissions consumption, organizations can identify areas for improvement and set more ambitious sustainability goals. According to a report by Raut et al. (2020), data analytics can help companies optimize their operations and comply with environmental regulations more effectively.

In addition, predictive analytics tools can forecast the environmental impact of different operational decisions. This allows companies to assess the consequences of their actions before implementing them, ensuring that more sustainable decisions are made in the long term.

### Innovation in Production Processes

Digitization of the supply chain also fosters innovation in production processes. Companies can use technologies such as additive manufacturing (3D printing) to produce components more efficiently and with less material waste. This technique makes it possible to manufacture only what is needed, thereby reducing surplus production and minimizing waste (Kamble et al., 2020).

In addition, smart factories can automatically adjust production processes based on the data collected, optimizing the use of resources and reducing waste in real time. This not only improves efficiency, but also helps companies to be more agile and adaptive in the face of market demands.

### *Improving Corporate Social Responsibility*

The adoption of sustainable practices driven by Industry 4.0 also improves the corporate social responsibility (CSR) of companies. Consumers are increasingly aware of the environmental impact of their purchasing decisions and prefer to support brands that demonstrate a commitment to sustainability. By implementing eco-efficiency technologies, companies can highlight their sustainability efforts, enhancing their brand image and appealing to a wider audience (Porter & Kramer, 2011).

This is especially relevant at a time of increasingly stringent environmental regulations. Companies that proactively adopt sustainable practices are better prepared to comply with these regulations and avoid penalties, which in turn improves their competitive position in the marketplace.

### *Economic Savings and Sustainability*

Sustainability and eco-efficiency are not only beneficial for the environment, but can also result in significant savings for companies. Reduced resource consumption and waste minimization translate directly into lower operating costs. According to a study by Accenture (2019), companies that implement sustainable practices can see a return on investment (ROI) of up to 40% on energy efficiency and waste reduction initiatives.

These savings can be reinvested in innovation and new product development, creating a positive cycle that benefits both the company and the environment. Investing in digital technologies for sustainability is not only an ethical imperative, but also a financially smart strategy.

## Challenges in Implementing Sustainable Technologies

Despite the benefits, implementing sustainable technologies in Industry 4.0 presents challenges. Companies must overcome technological, organizational and cultural barriers to effectively integrate these technologies into their operations. Lack of knowledge and experience in the use of digital technologies can be a significant obstacle (Kamble et al., 2020).

In addition, data security is a major concern. As companies collect and analyze large amounts of data, they must ensure that information is protected against cyberattacks and vulnerabilities. Investment in cybersecurity is essential to safeguard both operational data and consumer confidence in the company's sustainable practices.

### Data Driven Decision Making

The ability to leverage data analytics for better decision making is one of the most significant impacts of Industry 4.0 on supply chains. In a business environment characterized by dynamism and constant changes in consumer preferences, the use of data has become a key factor for competitiveness. Companies that integrate data analytics technologies into their operations are able to make more informed and strategic decisions, enabling them to improve their performance and adapt quickly to market conditions.

#### *Real Time Market Intelligence*

Companies use real-time market intelligence to model customer behaviors and anticipate their needs. This is achieved by collecting and analyzing data from a variety of sources, such as social networks, surveys and online transactions. By having access to up-to-date information on consumer preferences, organizations can adjust their marketing and product development strategies, ensuring that they meet market demands more effectively (Chae, 2019).

#### *Demand Forecasting*

The ability to predict demand more accurately is another key benefit of data analytics. Using advanced machine learning algorithms, companies can analyze historical sales patterns, seasonal trends and other factors that influence demand. This allows them to adjust their inventory and production levels, avoiding both overstocking and product shortages. According to a study by Waller et al. (2014), companies that implement predictive analytics tools can reduce inventory costs by 20-30%, resulting in a significant improvement in operational efficiency.

### *Inventory Level Optimization*

Optimizing inventory levels is crucial to improving customer service. By using real-time data to manage inventory, companies can ensure that products are available when customers demand them, which improves customer satisfaction and fosters brand loyalty. In addition, efficient inventory management also enables companies to reduce costs associated with warehousing and product obsolescence (Kamble et al., 2020).

### Production Scheduling

Machine learning algorithms not only improve demand forecasting, but also facilitate production scheduling. By analyzing data on resource availability, production capacities and lead times, companies can optimize their production lines to maximize efficiency and minimize downtime. This is especially important in lean production environments, where every minute of downtime can result in significant losses (Chae, 2019).

### *Maintenance Planning*

Maintenance planning is another area where data analytics plays a key role. Predictive maintenance technologies use sensor data and real-time monitoring to anticipate equipment failures before they occur. This allows companies to schedule maintenance in a way that minimizes disruptions to production, improving operational resilience and asset availability (Lee et al., 2014).

### *Adaptation to Market Fluctuations*

The ability to adapt quickly to market fluctuations is essential in Industry 4.0. Companies that use data analytics can react nimbly to changes in demand, adjusting their operations to meet new conditions. This enables them not only to survive in the face of market fluctuations, but also to take advantage of emerging opportunities that might have gone unnoticed without proper analytics (Raut et al., 2020).

### *Continuous Improvement through Data Analysis*

Data analytics also fosters a culture of continuous improvement within organizations. As companies collect more data and analyze it, they can identify areas for improvement in their operational processes. This applies not only to the supply chain, but also to other areas of the business, such as human resources and customer service. Constant data-driven feedback allows companies to adapt and evolve in an ever-changing business environment (Kamble et al., 2020).

## Challenges in Data-Driven Decision Making

Despite the benefits, implementing data-driven decision making also presents challenges. Companies must ensure they have the right infrastructure in place to collect and analyze large volumes of data. This includes investing in big data technologies and analytical skills within the workforce. Data security is also a major concern, as companies must protect sensitive information against cyberattacks and security breaches (Kamble et al., 2020).

## Challenges in the Implementation of Industry 4.0 in Supply Chains.

The implementation of Industry 4.0 technologies in supply chains presents a number of challenges that organizations must address to fully realize the potential benefits. These challenges can be categorized into technological, organizational and market-related issues. Despite the successful integration of Industry 4.0 technologies, many companies face challenges during implementation. A case analysis identified common problems, such as siloed operations and lack of alignment between information technology and operational technology (Kamble et al., 2020).

### *Technological Challenges*

One of the main challenges companies face is the integration of advanced technologies into their existing systems. Lack of interoperability between legacy systems and new solutions can limit organizations' ability to implement Industry 4.0 technologies effectively. The integration of IoT devices, data analytics platforms, and supply chain management systems requires a robust technology infrastructure that many companies do not yet possess (Kamble et al., 2020).

In addition, cybersecurity becomes a critical concern as companies digitize their operations. The interconnection of devices and systems increases the attack surface, exposing organizations to security risks. Implementing appropriate cybersecurity measures is essential to protect sensitive data and ensure operational continuity (Kamble et al., 2020).

### *Organizational Challenges*

Organizational challenges also play an important role in the implementation of

Industry 4.0. Many companies face internal resistance to change, which can hinder the adoption of new technologies. Organizational culture and employee mindset are critical aspects that must be considered. Organizations must foster a culture of innovation and continuous learning to facilitate the transition to a digital environment (Hazen et al., 2014).

The lack of technical skills and knowledge among personnel is another significant obstacle. Successful implementation of advanced technologies requires trained personnel who can manage and operate these systems. Companies must invest in training and skills development to prepare their workforce for the digital future (Wang et al., 2016).

### *Market-Related Challenges*

In the market context, companies also face significant challenges. Rapidly evolving technology and changing customer expectations require organizations to adapt quickly. However, many companies struggle to keep up with technological advances and market demands. This misalignment can result in a lack of competitiveness and missed business opportunities (Chae, 2019).

Economic uncertainty and fluctuations in market demand can further complicate the implementation of Industry 4.0 technologies. Companies must be able to anticipate and react to these changes, which requires flexibility and agility that are often not present in traditional organizational structures (Kamble et al., 2020).

### *Lack of Strategic Vision*

A critical challenge in implementing Industry 4.0 is the lack of a clear strategic vision. Many organizations approach digitization in a piecemeal fashion, without a comprehensive plan to guide their efforts. This lack of direction can result in ineffective investments and the implementation of technologies that do not align with overall business objectives (Hazen et al., 2014).

The lack of committed leadership and a well-defined strategy can lead to Industry 4.0 initiatives becoming isolated projects, rather than an integral part of the business strategy. Companies must establish a clear roadmap for digital transformation, ensuring that all stakeholders are aligned and committed to the goals (Kamble et al., 2020).

***Solution Scalability***

Another significant challenge is the scalability of implemented solutions. While a technology may work well on a small scale, its performance may suffer as it expands throughout the organization. Companies must consider how to scale their solutions effectively, ensuring that they can support increased production and operational complexity (Chae, 2019).

Advance planning and investment in adequate infrastructure are critical to address this problem. Companies should carefully assess their capabilities and needs before implementing new technologies, which will allow them to scale sustainably and effectively (Kamble et al., 2020).

**Collaboration with Supply Chain Partners**

Effective collaboration with supply chain partners is essential for the successful implementation of Industry 4.0. However, many companies find it difficult to integrate their systems with those of their suppliers and customers. The lack of common standards and communication protocols can hinder collaboration and process integration (Hazen et al., 2014).

Companies should work closely with partners to develop interoperable solutions that facilitate communication and data sharing. The creation of collaborative ecosystems can improve the efficiency and effectiveness of the supply chain, enabling organizations to take full advantage of the opportunities offered by Industry 4.0 (Wang et al., 2016).

### Strategic Challenges and Recommendations

To address these challenges, it is recommended that companies focus on building a minimum viable architecture that allows for gradual deployment and adjustment based on real-world feedback. By prioritizing the identification of immediate opportunities for impact, companies can build momentum for their digital transformation efforts, as demonstrated by organizations that successfully navigated these complexities (Wang et al., 2016). Staff training and change management are also critical aspects that must be considered to ensure a smooth transition to Industry 4.0.

#### *Prioritization of Immediate Opportunities*

Prioritizing the identification of immediate opportunities for impact is critical. Companies must evaluate their current operations and determine where Industry 4.0 technologies can generate quick and tangible benefits. This may include automating processes, improving inventory tracking, or optimizing logistics (Chae, 2019).

By focusing on areas that offer a relatively quick return on investment (ROI), companies can build momentum in their digital transformation efforts. This approach not only improves operational efficiency, but also provides a success story that can be used to gain additional support within the organization.

### *Staff Training*

Employee training is a critical aspect of a smooth transition to Industry 4.0. As companies implement new technologies, it is essential that employees understand how to use them effectively. This includes not only technical training, but also the development of soft skills, such as adaptability and teamwork (Hazen et al., 2014).

Organizations should invest in ongoing training programs that not only teach employees about new technologies, but also foster a mindset of innovation and continuous improvement. This will help prepare the workforce for the changes ahead and facilitate the adoption of new tools and processes.

### *Change Management*

Change management is another essential component of a successful Industry 4.0 implementation. Resistance to change is a common challenge in organizations, and it is crucial to address employee concerns proactively. This involves clearly communicating the benefits of the digital transformation and how it will positively affect each team member (Wang et al., 2016).

An effective approach to change management includes the creation of dedicated change teams that can guide the organization through the transformation process. These teams can provide support and resources, as well as be a channel for employee feedback, which helps adjust the approach as needed.

### Promotion of Innovation Culture

Fostering a culture of innovation within the organization is vital for the successful adoption of Industry 4.0. Companies should encourage employees to experiment and propose new ideas without fear of failure. This can be achieved by implementing incentives and recognition programs that reward innovation and creativity (Hazen et al., 2014).

A culture of innovation not only improves employee morale, but can also result in creative solutions to complex problems. By empowering employees to be part of the transformation process, companies can benefit from a greater diversity of ideas and approaches.

### Establishment of Strategic Alliances

Establishing strategic alliances with technology providers and other relevant industry players can facilitate the implementation of Industry 4.0. These collaborations can provide access to expertise, advanced technologies and best practices that can accelerate the transformation process (Kamble et al., 2020).

Companies should seek partnerships that complement their internal capabilities and help them overcome technological and knowledge limitations. Working with strategic partners allows organizations to share risks and resources, which can result in a more successful implementation.

### Performance Evaluation and Measurement

Performance evaluation and measurement are critical to ensure that digital transformation efforts are aligned with business objectives. Companies must establish clear metrics and KPIs that allow them to monitor the progress and impact of Industry 4.0 technologies (Chae, 2019).

Collecting operational performance data and employee feedback will help organizations identify areas for improvement and adjust their strategies as needed. This practice of continuous evaluation also demonstrates the company's commitment to improvement and adaptability.

**Flexibility and Adaptability**

Finally, companies must adopt a mindset of flexibility and adaptability. The business environment is constantly changing, and organizations that can quickly adjust their strategies and operations will be better positioned to thrive in the digital age. This involves not only being open to new technologies, but also being responsive to market feedback and changing consumer needs (Wang et al., 2016).

Companies that foster a culture of learning and adaptation can more easily navigate the challenges of Industry 4.0 implementation and make the most of the opportunities that arise.

# Chapter 3: Challenges and Opportunities in the Implementation of Industry 4.0

The implementation of Industry 4.0 (I 4.0) represents a significant change in industrial practices, introducing multifaceted dynamics involving the integration of advanced technologies into manufacturing processes. This concept, rooted in the Fourth Industrial Revolution, highlights how digital innovations such as artificial intelligence (AI), the Internet of Things (IoT) and cloud computing combine to create intelligent and automated manufacturing environments (Kamble et al., 2020).

### Implementation Challenges

The transition to I 4.0 presents a number of challenges that organizations must overcome to successfully adopt and implement these advanced technologies.

### Financial Barriers

One of the main obstacles in the implementation of Industry 4.0 (I 4.0) is the high initial investment required and the uncertainty related to the return on investment (ROI). This situation is compounded by the perceived risk associated with emerging technologies. Many organizations find it difficult to justify the upfront costs of implementing advanced technologies, especially when the financial benefits may not be immediate. As Waller and Fawcett (2014) point out, this hesitancy can deter companies from moving toward needed changes, particularly in competitive environments where adaptability is essential.

Lack of clarity about ROI can lead to conservative decisions, where companies prefer to maintain their legacy systems rather than invest in new technologies. This phenomenon is common in industries where profit margins are tight and pressure to reduce costs is constant. Organizations may be afraid to commit significant capital to initiatives that do not guarantee immediate results, which can result in a loss of competitiveness compared to those that do make the investment (Kamble et al., 2020).

In addition, the financial uncertainty associated with I 4.0 can be particularly daunting for small and medium-sized enterprises (SMEs), which often have limited resources. These organizations may lack the capacity to absorb high upfront costs, putting them at a competitive disadvantage against larger, more investment-intensive companies. As a result, SMEs may miss out on innovation opportunities that could have improved their efficiency and adaptability (Hazen et al., 2014).

To overcome these financial barriers, organizations should consider alternative financing strategies, such as public-private partnerships or specific investment funds for technological innovation. In addition, it is essential to conduct a thorough cost-benefit analysis that not only evaluates short-term economic benefits, but also considers long-term benefits, such as improved product quality and customer satisfaction. This can help companies visualize the added value that I 4.0 can bring to their operations.

Finally, training and workforce development are investments that must also be considered within the financial framework. Investing in skills and knowledge can be a key factor in maximizing the ROI of I 4.0. According to Kusiak (2018), organizations that invest in workforce training not only increase their ability to implement advanced technologies, but also foster a culture of innovation that can result in sustainable growth and long-term competitive advantage. In short, addressing financial barriers involves a strategic approach that considers investments not only in technology, but also in human capital.

### Technology Integration

Effective integration of technologies into existing systems and workflows is both imperative and complex for organizations looking to implement Industry 4.0 (I 4.0). Adopting new technologies not only requires significant financial investment, but also involves cultural and organizational change. Companies must select appropriate suppliers and ensure that emerging technologies are seamlessly integrated into their operations. This makes integration planning and execution critical processes that require careful attention (Kamble et al., 2020).

One of the most important challenges in technology integration is the lack of standardized data formats. In an industrial environment where multiple systems and devices must communicate with each other, the absence of common standards can create information silos. This not only hinders collaboration and data sharing, but can also lead to errors in decision making. As Waller and Fawcett (2014) point out, interoperability is essential to capitalize on the capabilities of advanced technologies, and the lack of standards can be a considerable obstacle.

In addition, incompatible interfaces between different systems can further complicate integration. Many organizations operate with legacy systems that are not designed to interface with new I 4.0 technologies. This misalignment can result in a fragmented implementation, where technologies do not work cohesively, limiting the potential for improved efficiency and productivity (Hazen et al., 2014). To overcome this challenge, it is critical that companies conduct a thorough inventory of their existing systems and assess how new technologies can be effectively incorporated.

Vendor selection also plays a crucial role in the success of technology integration. Organizations should consider not only the quality of the technologies offered, but also the vendor's ability to offer technical support and training. Collaborating with suppliers that have experience in implementing I 4.0 solutions can ease the process and reduce the downtime associated with transitioning to new technologies (Kusiak, 2018). Establishing strong and trusting relationships with suppliers is essential to ensure a smooth implementation.

Staff training is another critical aspect of the integration process. Lack of adequate skills within the workforce can become a major impediment. Organizations should invest in training programs that enable their employees to develop the necessary competencies to manage and operate new technologies. This not only increases implementation efficiency, but also promotes a culture of innovation and continuous improvement (Raut et al., 2020).

In addition, technology integration should be viewed as a continuous process rather than a one-time event. As technologies evolve and new tools emerge, organizations must be prepared to adapt their systems and processes. This involves not only upgrading existing technologies, but also reviewing and improving workflows to maximize efficiency (Chae, 2019). Organizational flexibility and agility are key to maintaining competitiveness in an ever-changing environment.

Finally, change management is a critical aspect that is often overlooked in the integration process. Organizations must recognize that the adoption of new technologies can generate resistance among employees. Establishing clear communication about the benefits of integration and providing adequate support during the transition can help mitigate this resistance. Involving employees in the change process and fostering an inclusive environment can facilitate a more successful and sustainable integration (Porter & Kramer, 2011).

### Skilled Labor

The availability of skilled labor is a critical challenge in the implementation of Industry 4.0 (I 4.0). There is a considerable gap between the capabilities of the current workforce and the skills required to operate advanced technologies. This disparity has become a significant obstacle for organizations seeking to adopt emerging technologies, as the lack of skilled personnel can limit their ability to maximize the potential of I 4.0 (Kusiak, 2018).

To address this gap, organizations must invest in training and professional development programs. Ongoing training is essential to equip employees with the skills needed to effectively manage and use new technologies. This involves not only technical training on specific tools, but also developing competencies in data analytics, cybersecurity and complex systems management. By doing so, companies can foster a culture of innovation and adaptability that allows them to remain competitive in a constantly evolving industrial environment (Raut et al., 2020).

In addition, organizations should consider collaborating with educational institutions and training centers to create training programs aligned with market needs.

These collaborations can facilitate the creation of a pipeline of qualified talent ready to meet the challenges of I 4.0. This not only closes skills gaps, but also strengthens the relationship between the industrial and educational sector, which is beneficial for both parties (Chae, 2019).

### Technology Upgrade and Sustainability

Organizations looking to implement Industry 4.0 (I 4.0) must be prepared to continuously upgrade their technologies. The rapid evolution of digital tools and systems requires companies to not only make significant financial investments, but also develop sound strategic planning. This planning is vital to ensure that technological changes are aligned with broader organizational goals, enabling companies to remain competitive in an ever-changing environment (Kamble et al., 2020).

Technological upgrading should not be considered an isolated event, but a continuous process that is integrated into the organizational culture. Companies should establish a framework that facilitates the regular evaluation of their systems and technologies, ensuring that they remain relevant and effective. This includes identifying new trends in the industry and evaluating how these can be adopted to improve operational efficiency and product quality (Chae, 2019). Adopting a proactive approach towards technology upgrades allows organizations to quickly adapt to market demands and changing customer expectations.

In addition, sustainability has become a crucial aspect in the implementation of I 4.0. Organizations must consider the efficient use of resources as an integral part of their technology strategies. The integration of sustainable practices not only helps to reduce costs in the long run, but also improves the company's reputation and its relationship with stakeholders. According to Raut et al. (2020), companies that implement sustainable technologies can benefit from greater market acceptance and competitive advantage over those that do not.

The implementation of sustainable technologies can include the digitization of processes to optimize the use of energy and resources, as well as the adoption of circular business models that minimize waste. This transition to more sustainable practices is not only beneficial for the environment, but can also result in significant improvements in operational efficiency. Organizations that prioritize sustainability often find that they can reduce their operating costs while complying with increasingly stringent environmental regulations (Kusiak, 2018).

Finally, to achieve successful technology upgrades and sustainability, organizations must foster a culture of innovation and continuous learning. This involves empowering employees to adapt to new technologies and sustainable approaches, as well as encouraging cross-departmental collaboration to find innovative solutions. Creating an environment where employees feel valued and empowered to contribute to sustainability and innovation will enable organizations to not only achieve their short-term goals, but also ensure their long-term success in the era of I 4.0.

## Implementation Opportunities

### *Competitive Advantage through Technology Acquisition*

Successful implementation of Industry 4.0 (I 4.0) presents organizations with substantial opportunities to gain competitive advantage through the effective adoption of new technologies. This process begins with identifying customer needs and analyzing the organization's business model. By understanding what customers value and how the value proposition can be improved, companies can select technologies that truly impact their performance and customer satisfaction (Kamble et al., 2020).

Once customer needs have been identified, the next step is to evaluate how emerging technologies can be integrated into existing processes to meet those needs. For example, the use of artificial intelligence (AI) and data analytics can provide valuable information that enables companies to anticipate market trends and adjust their offerings accordingly. This ability to respond quickly to customer demands translates into significant competitive differentiation (Chae, 2019).

In addition, the adoption of advanced technologies enables organizations to optimize their internal operations. Process automation, for example, can lead to greater efficiency and cost reduction, enabling companies to offer more competitive prices. The implementation of IoT technology can improve visibility into the supply chain, which facilitates inventory management and waste reduction (Raut et al., 2020). In this way, organizations not only improve their profitability, but also strengthen their market position.

Mass customization is another key opportunity that I 4.0 offers companies. By using flexible manufacturing technologies, organizations can tailor their products to individual customer preferences. This capability not only satisfies the demand for customization, but also fosters customer loyalty by providing solutions that align more closely with their expectations (Bai et al., 2019). Personalization becomes a crucial differentiator in an increasingly saturated market.

The integration of digital technologies also enables companies to innovate their business models. For example, the subscription economy has gained popularity in a variety of industries, from software to physical products. By adopting subscription-based business models, companies can generate recurring revenue streams and improve customer retention. This requires a deep understanding of how digital technologies can facilitate these transitions (Kusiak, 2018).

In addition, the ability to collect and analyze large volumes of data enables companies to make more informed and strategic decisions. Predictive analytics tools can help organizations anticipate changes in demand or identify new market opportunities. This not only improves agility, but also allows companies to position themselves proactively rather than reactively, which is crucial in volatile market environments (Waller & Fawcett, 2014).

However, to maximize these opportunities, organizations must ensure that their technology infrastructure is ready to support I 4.0 implementation. This includes not only adopting new technologies, but also upgrading existing systems to ensure interoperability and efficiency. Lack of adequate infrastructure can limit the ability of companies to take full advantage of the competitive advantages that I 4.0 offers (Hazen et al., 2014).

Collaboration with technology partners is also critical in this context. Companies that work with suppliers and strategic partners that have experience in implementing advanced technologies can benefit from shared knowledge and best practices. This collaboration not only facilitates the integration of new technologies, but can also open up new market opportunities and improve product and service offerings (Kamble et al., 2020).

Finally, organizational culture plays a crucial role in a company's ability to take advantage of the opportunities associated with I 4.0. Fostering an environment that values innovation, experimentation and continuous learning is essential for success. Organizations that cultivate an open mindset toward change and technology are better positioned to adapt and thrive in the Industry 4.0 era (Porter & Kramer, 2011).

In summary, the implementation of I 4.0 offers organizations significant opportunities to gain competitive advantage through the effective adoption of new technologies. From mass customization to process optimization and business model innovation, companies that invest in these emerging technologies can differentiate themselves in an increasingly competitive marketplace.

### Mass Customization

Industry 4.0 (I 4.0) enables organizations to offer mass customization of products, effectively responding to the growing demand for personalized solutions. In an increasingly competitive marketplace, consumers are looking for products that not only meet their basic needs, but also align with their individual preferences. The ability to tailor products according to these preferences not only improves customer satisfaction, but also fosters brand loyalty by creating a deeper connection between consumer and producer (Chae, 2019).

Mass customization relies on the integration of advanced technologies such as artificial intelligence (AI), the Internet of Things (IoT) and additive manufacturing. These technologies enable companies to collect and analyze real-time data on consumer preferences and behaviors. By better understanding what their customers want, organizations can offer personalized options that go beyond standard configurations, thus creating a more engaging and relevant shopping experience (Kamble et al., 2020).

One of the keys to implementing mass customization is flexibility on the production line. Advanced manufacturing technologies allow companies to quickly adjust their processes to accommodate variations in orders without compromising efficiency. For example, 3D printers can produce customized parts on demand, reducing the lead time and costs associated with mass production. This flexibility not only responds to customer expectations, but also optimizes the supply chain by minimizing inventory (Raut et al., 2020).

In addition, mass customization can lead to greater innovation in product development. By allowing consumers to participate in the design process, companies can gain valuable feedback on what they really want. This co-creation not only improves the quality of the final product, but also creates a sense of ownership among consumers, who feel more connected to the brand. Direct feedback from customers can drive a continuous cycle of innovation and improvement (Bai et al., 2019).

However, implementing mass customization also poses significant challenges. Organizations must ensure that their management systems are robust enough to handle the complexity involved in customizing products on a large scale. This involves not only integrating advanced technologies, but also training the workforce to manage these processes (Kusiak, 2018). Without proper planning, companies can face difficulties that limit their ability to deliver personalization effectively.

Customer experience is another crucial aspect of mass customization. Companies should focus on how these personalized options are perceived by the consumer. The ease of use of personalization platforms, as well as clarity in communicating the available options, are factors that can influence the purchase decision. An intuitive and engaging user experience can significantly increase conversion rate and customer satisfaction (Chae, 2019).

Finally, mass customization is not only about meeting consumer demands, but also about doing so in a sustainable way. Organizations must consider the environmental impact of producing customized products. Through the use of efficient production technologies and sustainable materials, companies can not only meet consumer expectations for customization, but also do so in a way that minimizes their ecological footprint (Raut et al., 2020). In this way, mass customization becomes a strategy that not only benefits consumers, but also promotes responsible and sustainable business practices.

### Strategic Application of Technology

The strategic application of Industry 4.0 (I 4.0) technologies provides a solid foundation for differentiation or cost leadership, enabling companies to compete more efficiently in the marketplace. As organizations adopt advanced technologies, they can optimize their processes and improve the quality of their products, resulting in a more attractive value proposition for consumers. This approach not only improves operational efficiency, but also opens up new opportunities for product and service innovation (Kamble et al., 2020).

One of the keys to developing a sustainable competitive advantage is the creation of unique technological capabilities that are difficult for competitors to replicate. Investments in technologies such as artificial intelligence, machine learning and process automation enable organizations not only to improve their efficiency, but also to offer products and services that are tailored to the specific needs of their customers. This customization and flexibility in offerings are critical factors that can differentiate a company in a saturated market (Chae, 2019).

In addition, real-time data collection and analysis enables companies to make more informed and agile decisions. By using advanced analytics technologies, organizations can identify emerging trends and respond quickly to changing market demands. This not only improves adaptability, but also fosters an organizational culture that values agility and continuous innovation (Waller & Fawcett, 2014). Companies that manage to integrate this data into their strategy can anticipate customer needs and adjust their operations accordingly.

The strategic application of technology also involves regularly evaluating strategies to ensure that they are aligned with market trends and customer expectations. Organizations must establish feedback mechanisms that allow them to measure the effectiveness of their technology initiatives and make timely adjustments. This continuous evaluation is crucial to stay relevant in a rapidly changing business environment (Porter & Kramer, 2011).

In addition, organizations must consider the impact of technologies on their supply chains. I 4.0 enables greater visibility and traceability, which can result in more efficient resource management and reduced costs. Implementing technologies such as the Internet of Things (IoT) in the supply chain allows companies to monitor in real time the status of products and optimize logistics processes, which contributes to greater efficiency and waste reduction (Hazen et al., 2014).

Training and workforce development are also essential components of strategic technology implementation. Organizations must invest in training to equip their employees with the skills needed to operate and manage new technologies. This not only enhances workforce capability, but also fosters a culture of continuous learning that is vital for innovation and adaptation in an ever-changing technology environment (Kusiak, 2018).

Collaboration with strategic and technology partners can also be a critical factor in the successful implementation of I 4.0. Working together with technology providers and platforms allows organizations to access knowledge and resources that can accelerate the adoption of new technologies. This collaboration can also facilitate the sharing of best practices and the creation of innovative solutions that benefit all parties involved (Raut et al., 2020).

Sustainability is another important aspect to consider in the strategic application of technology. Organizations that implement sustainable practices in their operations not only meet consumer expectations, but can also reduce costs and enhance their brand image. Integrating technologies that optimize resource use and minimize environmental impact can be a significant competitive advantage in today's environmentally conscious economy (Bai et al., 2019).

Finally, organizational culture plays a crucial role in the effectiveness of the strategic application of technology. Fostering an environment that values innovation and change can facilitate the adoption of new technologies and the achievement of strategic objectives. Companies that promote experimentation and openness to change are better positioned to take advantage of the opportunities presented by I 4.0 and ultimately ensure their long-term success in an ever-changing marketplace (Kamble et al., 2020).

In summary, the strategic application of I 4.0 technologies not only provides a sustainable competitive advantage, but also enables organizations to adapt to an ever-changing business environment. By integrating these technologies into their operations and strategies, companies can optimize their performance, meet customer demands and prepare for the future.

# Chapter 4: Education and Training in the Age of Industry 4.0

Education and training in the era of Industry 4.0 is undergoing a crucial transformation, where educational frameworks and training programs must adapt to prepare people for a rapidly evolving workforce. The Fourth Industrial Revolution, characterized by the integration of advanced technologies such as artificial intelligence (AI), the Internet of Things (IoT) and robotics, requires a re-evaluation of traditional educational methodologies. This change is essential to address the growing skills gap in critical areas such as digital literacy, critical thinking, and problem solving, which are fundamental in an increasingly digital and interconnected economy (Kamble et al., 2020).

Educational institutions are adopting innovative pedagogical approaches, such as Education 4.0, which emphasizes experiential learning, interdisciplinary studies and technological integration. These strategies seek to develop competencies necessary for success in a modern work environment, reflecting the importance of education as a driver of economic competitiveness and social progress. However, the transition to these new models faces significant challenges, including resistance to change in education systems and lack of alignment between curricula and industry needs (Chae, 2019).

The digital divide stands as a major obstacle, limiting access to technology and educational resources for disadvantaged populations, especially in the wake of the COVID-19 pandemic. To overcome these challenges, it is crucial to foster continued collaboration between educational institutions and industry stakeholders. This cooperation will ensure that training programs remain relevant and effective, preparing students for future challenges (Bai et al., 2019). In summary, the educational landscape of the Industry 4.0 era represents a vital intersection between technology and learning, driving a paradigm shift that seeks to equip students with the skills needed to thrive in an automated, data-driven world.

### Impacts on Education

The emergence of Industry 4.0 has profound implications for education, requiring a paradigm shift in teaching and learning methodologies. This phenomenon, characterized by the integration of advanced technologies such as artificial intelligence, robotics and the Internet of Things, is transforming not only how goods and services are produced, but also how they are taught and learned. As technology evolves, the gap between traditional educational practices and the skills in demand in the workforce is widening, especially in areas such as critical thinking, creativity, and technological competence (Kusiak, 2018).

One of the main challenges facing education in the Industry 4.0 era is the need to update curricula to align them with the competencies required in the labor market. Educational institutions must adopt pedagogical approaches that integrate technology and encourage active learning. This implies not only the incorporation of digital tools, but also the creation of learning environments that promote collaboration and innovation (Chae, 2019). Education must evolve towards a model that prepares students to solve complex problems and adapt to a constantly changing work environment.

In addition, the digital divide represents a significant obstacle to the implementation of these new methodologies. Many populations, especially in rural or disadvantaged areas, lack access to the technology necessary to fully participate in modern education. This not only limits learning opportunities, but also perpetuates existing inequalities in access to quality education (Bai et al., 2019). Therefore, it is crucial that education policies include strategies to close this gap and ensure that all students have access to the necessary tools and resources.

Collaboration between educational institutions and industry is critical to ensure that training programs remain relevant and effective. This cooperation can manifest itself in the creation of internship programs, joint projects, and the development of curricula that reflect the needs of the labor market (Raut et al., 2020). By working together, educational institutions can tailor their offerings to prepare students not only with theoretical knowledge, but also with practical skills that are directly applicable in the work environment.

It is also essential that teachers receive continuous training in digital competencies and innovative pedagogical methodologies. Educator training is a key component for the successful implementation of educational reforms in the Industry 4.0 era. Teachers must be equipped not only with technical knowledge, but also with skills to foster critical and creative learning among their students (Waller & Fawcett, 2014). This includes the ability to use emerging technologies in the classroom and to guide students in developing interpersonal and problem-solving skills.

Finally, research and innovation must be pillars in contemporary education. Educational institutions must commit to continually researching best practices and adapting their approaches based on emerging trends in technology and the labor market. This will not only ensure that educational programs are relevant, but will also enable students to develop a continuous learning mindset, essential in a rapidly changing world of work (Kamble et al., 2020).

### Educational Reforms and Frameworks

To address the disparity between the skills required in the labor market and those taught in educational institutions, it is essential to design educational frameworks that are aligned with the needs of a constantly evolving work environment. Industry 4.0 has transformed not only production processes, but also the skills required for workers. Therefore, educational frameworks must adapt to incorporate skills such as digital literacy, critical thinking and problem-solving skills, which are essential in a highly automated and technological work context (Kamble et al., 2020).

In addition, these frameworks should promote scientific and ethical development, ensuring that students are not only competent in technical skills, but also in ethical values that guide their professional behavior. Education must foster a critical mindset that enables students to question, investigate and make informed decisions. This is especially relevant in a world where information is abundant but not always accurate, requiring future professionals to discern between different sources and perspectives (Chae, 2019).

The integration of Education 4.0 components is crucial to prepare students for the challenges of the future. This involves adopting teaching methodologies that promote collaborative learning and hands-on experience, rather than relying solely on traditional lecture-based teaching. The use of emerging technologies, such as augmented reality and digital simulation, can enrich the educational process, offering students opportunities to interact with content more dynamically and effectively (Waller & Fawcett, 2014).

The Sustainable Development Goals (SDGs), and in particular SDG 4, underline the need for inclusive and equitable quality education. This goal has become even more urgent in the aftermath of the COVID-19 pandemic, which exacerbated existing inequalities in access to education. The health crisis has highlighted that educational institutions must be resilient and able to adapt to adverse situations, ensuring that all students, regardless of their socioeconomic background, have access to quality learning opportunities (UNESCO, 2020).

To achieve these educational reforms, it is essential to foster collaboration between educational institutions, governments and industry sectors. This cooperation can facilitate the development of curricula that reflect emerging trends in the labor market and ensure that students are equipped with the skills necessary to thrive in an ever-changing work environment. In addition, ongoing teacher training in new technologies and pedagogies is vital to ensure that they can implement these reforms effectively (Raut et al., 2020). The education of the future must be a joint effort that prepares new generations to face the challenges of the digital age.

**Technology Integration**

Incorporating technology into educational environments is essential to prepare students for the challenges of Industry 4.0. Rapid technological evolution requires educational institutions to transform their teaching and learning methods. This includes implementing digital and analytics tools that not only enhance the educational experience, but also enable educators to monitor and predict student outcomes with greater accuracy (Kamble et al., 2020). This technology integration can facilitate learning that is more tailored to individual needs, promoting a more personalized approach.

One of the most prominent resources in modern education is massive open online courses (MOOCs). These courses allow thousands of students to access high quality educational content from anywhere in the world, breaking geographical and economic barriers. According to Hazen et al. (2014), MOOCs not only benefit students, but also educators, who can update their knowledge and skills through platforms that offer continuous training. This accessibility is crucial in a world where education must be inclusive and equitable.

In addition to MOOCs, technology can facilitate the use of learning management platforms (LMS), which allow educators to organize and distribute content, as well as interact with students more effectively. These platforms can include analytics tools that provide data on student performance, which helps identify areas for improvement and adapt instruction accordingly (Waller & Fawcett, 2014). The ability to track student progress in real time is a significant advantage offered by technology in education.

Pedagogical practices must also evolve to incorporate active learning skills, which are essential to prepare students for the modern workforce. Active learning involves students actively participating in their learning process through methods such as project-based learning, group discussions and simulations. This approach encourages not only the acquisition of knowledge, but also the development of interpersonal and problem-solving skills (Kusiak, 2018).

Critical thinking, a skill increasingly in demand in the workplace, must also be an integral component of modern education. Technology can facilitate this development by providing students with access to a wide range of information and resources. However, it is the responsibility of educators to guide students in critically evaluating this information, helping them to discern between reliable and unreliable sources (Bai et al., 2019). Fostering critical thinking is essential to prepare students to meet the complex challenges presented by the digital age.

Gamification is another strategy that can be integrated into learning to increase learner motivation and engagement. By incorporating game elements into the educational process, such as points, levels and rewards, the learning experience can be transformed into something more engaging and dynamic. This methodology not only improves knowledge retention, but also promotes teamwork and healthy competition among students (Raut et al., 2020).

Likewise, augmented reality (AR) and virtual reality (VR) are emerging as powerful tools in education, offering immersive experiences that can enrich learning. These technologies allow students to explore complex concepts in a visual and hands-on way, facilitating understanding of topics that might otherwise be abstract. For example, in fields such as medicine or engineering, AR and VR can simulate real-world situations, giving students the opportunity to practice and learn in a safe environment (Chae, 2019).

However, the integration of technology in education is not without its challenges. One of the main obstacles is the digital divide, which limits access to technology for many populations. The COVID-19 pandemic has highlighted these inequalities, showing that not all students have access to adequate devices or a reliable Internet connection. For technological integration to be effective, it is essential that policies are implemented to ensure equitable access to technological resources (UNESCO, 2020).

Finally, ongoing teacher training in the use of new technologies is essential for the success of these initiatives. Educators must be trained not only in the use of technological tools, but also in how to integrate them effectively into their pedagogical practices. This involves developing a solid understanding of how technology can be used to enhance learning and teaching, as well as keeping up with emerging trends in edtech (Kusiak, 2018).

In conclusion, the integration of technology in education is an essential process that can transform the way teaching and learning takes place. By implementing digital tools, encouraging active learning and critical thinking, and paying attention to equity in access, educational institutions can prepare students to thrive in an ever-changing work environment. Collaboration between educators, institutions and industry will be key to ensuring that these reforms are effective and sustainable over time.

### Interdisciplinary Approaches

The advent of Industry 4.0 has transformed the nature of work, requiring educational institutions to adopt interdisciplinary approaches in their programs. This approach is based on the integration of different disciplines to prepare students for work environments that are increasingly Collaborative and innovative. By designing programs that cross traditional knowledge boundaries, students are offered the opportunity to develop a broader and more relevant skill set aligned with the demands of the modern labor market (Kamble et al., 2020).

One of the main benefits of interdisciplinary approaches is the ability to foster critical thinking and creativity. In a world where problems are complex and multifaceted, students need to learn to approach challenges from multiple perspectives. By combining knowledge from diverse areas, such as engineering, computer science, social sciences, and art, students can develop innovative and effective solutions that would not be possible from a single discipline (Raut et al., 2020). This integration not only prepares students to solve specific problems, but also gives them the tools they need to adapt to changing situations in the future.

In addition, collaboration across disciplines can enrich the educational process by allowing students to work on real projects that reflect the challenges they will face in the working world. For example, a team composed of engineering, graphic design and marketing students might work together on product development, learning to communicate their ideas and integrate their different skills into a cohesive outcome. This type of hands-on experience not only reinforces academic learning, but also facilitates the development of interpersonal skills, such as communication and teamwork, which are essential in today's work environment (Kusiak, 2018).

Finally, it is essential that educational institutions foster a culture that values and promotes interdisciplinarity. This involves not only creating integrative curricula, but also training teachers to teach in interdisciplinary contexts and creating collaborative spaces that facilitate the exchange of ideas among students from different disciplines (Chae, 2019). By making interdisciplinarity a priority, educational institutions not only prepare students for success in a digital and interconnected world, but also contribute to the development of a more innovative and adaptable workforce.

### Training Approaches

Training programs designed for Industry 4.0 focus on accessibility and flexibility, critical elements to address the diverse needs of students and educators in an ever-changing work environment. In this context, it is essential that programs not only offer theoretical content, but also provide hands-on experiences that allow students to apply what they learn in real-world situations. This combination of theory and practice is critical to ensure that students are fully prepared to meet the challenges presented by the Fourth Industrial Revolution (Kamble et al., 2020).

One of the most effective strategies for achieving this accessibility and flexibility is the use of digital platforms that host learning resources. These information portals can include instructional materials, video tutorials, discussion forums, and interactive exercises, allowing learners to access a variety of resources that are tailored to their individual learning styles. In addition, these platforms can facilitate personalization of learning, allowing students to progress at their own pace and delve deeper into areas of particular interest (Hazen et al., 2014).

To facilitate hands-on learning, it is crucial that training programs integrate industrial software and technology tools that simulate real-world scenarios. This can include the use of simulators, computer-aided design (CAD) programs and data analysis platforms. These tools not only enhance understanding of complex concepts, but also allow students to acquire technical skills that are highly valued in the job market (Kusiak, 2018). Hands-on experience using these technologies prepares students to work with the systems they will encounter in their future careers.

In addition, collaboration with educational partners and participation in initiatives such as WorldSkills are essential components of these training programs. These partnerships allow educators and students to access additional resources and networking opportunities, as well as provide hands-on learning experiences that are difficult to replicate in a traditional classroom. WorldSkills, for example, organizes competitions that challenge students to demonstrate their skills in a competitive and collaborative environment, giving them valuable experience in applying their knowledge (Raut et al., 2020).

Continuous training of instructors is also a vital aspect of designing effective training programs. Educators must be trained in the latest technologies and pedagogical methodologies in order to effectively guide students. This involves not only becoming familiar with new tools and approaches, but also understanding how to integrate these technologies into their daily teaching to maximize student learning (Chae, 2019). Ongoing professional training ensures that instructors remain current and are able to deliver quality education.

In addition, constant evaluation and adjustment of training programs are crucial to their effectiveness. It is important for educational institutions to collect feedback from students and industry to identify areas for improvement and adapt to the changing demands of the labor market. This can include surveys, interviews, and performance analysis, which will help educators adjust their teaching methods and update program content as needed (Bai et al., 2019).

Finally, creating a culture of collaborative learning within training programs can further enrich the educational experience. Encouraging teamwork and the exchange of ideas among students from different disciplines not only improves interpersonal skills, but also promotes innovation and creativity. By working together on projects and challenges, students can learn from each other's experiences and perspectives, which better prepares them for work in a diverse and dynamic professional environment (Kamble et al., 2020).

**Future Directions**

As industries evolve in response to the demands of Industry 4.0, the need for the workforce to adapt their skills becomes increasingly urgent. Automation and emerging technologies are transforming the nature of work, meaning that many traditional skills may become obsolete. However, despite this automation, there are sectors that will continue to demand skilled labor, such as construction, maintenance and manufacturing. This trend presents valuable opportunities for workers to upgrade their skills and prepare for roles that will continue to be relevant in the future (Raut et al., 2020).

One of the sectors that will benefit considerably from this change is the construction industry. The implementation of technologies such as drones, building information modeling (BIM) and 3D printing is revolutionizing the way projects are planned and executed. These advances not only increase efficiency, but also require a new set of skills for operation and maintenance. Therefore, it is essential that training and education programs in this sector are updated to include these emerging technologies, preparing workers for roles that are not only technical, but also strategic (Kusiak, 2018).

In the field of maintenance, the digitization of equipment and the implementation of real-time monitoring technologies are changing the way preventive and predictive maintenance is carried out. Maintenance technicians must now be able to interpret analytical data and work with automated systems. This implies that educational institutions must offer programs that combine technical training with analytical and problem-solving skills, preparing students to perform in an increasingly digitized environment (Hazen et al., 2014).

Manufacturing is also undergoing a significant transformation, driven by the adoption of technologies such as collaborative robotics and artificial intelligence. As these technologies are integrated into production lines, workers will need to acquire skills that enable them to interact and work alongside advanced machines. This involves not only technical skills, but also the ability to adapt to a work environment that can change rapidly. Continuous training and retraining will be key to keeping the workforce up-to-date and competitive in this sector (Kamble et al., 2020).

In addition, the focus on sustainability and corporate social responsibility is creating new opportunities in sectors that were not previously considered. For example, the development of clean technologies and sustainable manufacturing practices is creating a demand for workers with skills in these areas. Educational institutions need to recognize this trend and develop programs that prepare students to work in a future that prioritizes sustainability, which in turn can help bridge the gap between education and labor market needs (Bai et al., 2019).

Finally, it is crucial that education and labor policies are aligned to facilitate the transition to an adaptive and well-prepared workforce. This includes collaboration between governments, educational institutions and industry to develop programs that respond to emerging labor market needs. In addition, a culture of lifelong learning must be promoted, where workers feel that they can update their skills throughout their careers.

# References

*Adame, T., Bel, A., Bellalta, B., Barcelo, J., Oliver, M., &Almirall, A. (2019). IncreasingLPWAN scalability by means of concurrent multiband IoT technologies: An industry 4.0 use case. IEEE Access, 7, 46990-47010. https://doi.org/10.1109/ACCESS.2019.2909608.*

*Agrawal, M., Eloot, K., Mancini, M., & Patel, A. (2020, July 29). Industry 4.0: Reimagining manufacturing operations after COVID-19. McKinsey & Company. https://www.mckinsey.com/capabilities/operations/our-insights/industry-40- reimagining-manufacturing-operations-after-covid-19.*

*Alaloul, W. S. S., Liew, M. S., Zawawi, N. A. W. A., & Kennedy, I. B. (2019). Industry revolution IR 4.0: Future opportunities and challenges in the construction industry. MATEC Web of Conferences, 203, 1-7. https://doi.org/10.1051/matecconf/201820302001.*

*Ateam Admin (2024, May 23). IoT in manufacturing industry: Transforming the way we make things " A-Team Global. A-Team Global. https://a-team.global/blog/iot-in-manufacturing-industry/*

*Bai, C., Sarkis, J., & Wang, Z. (2019). Green supply chain management in the context of Industry 4.0: A review andfuture research directions. Journal of Cleaner Production, 230, 10531068. https://doi.org/10.1016/j.jclepro.2019.05.279. https://doi.org/10.1016/j.jclepro.2019.05.279*

*Bennett, D., Desai, M., & Yeandle, D. (2017). Industry 4.0: Skills and training for the future workforce. International Journal of Engineering Education, 33(6), 1984-*

*1992.*

*Bessant, J., & Tidd, J. (2015). Innovation and entrepreneurship. Wiley.*

*Bonilla, S., Silva, H., Da Silva, M. T., Gonçalves, R. F., & Sacomano, J. (2018). Industry 4.0 and Sustainability Implications: A Scenario-Based Analysis of the Impacts and challenges. Sustainability, 10(10), 3740. https://doi.org/10.3390/su10103740.*

*Briceño, G., V. (2021, December 2). First Industrial Revolution | What it was, history, stages, causes, consequences. Euston96. https://www.euston96.com/en/first-industrial- revolution/*

*Brook, J. (n.d.). How Industry 4.0 Technologies can drive Manufacturing Productivity Growth.*

*FourJaw Manufacturing Analytics Ltd. https://fourjaw.com/blog/how-industry-4.0-technologies-can-drive-manufacturing-productivity-growth*

*Buyukozkan, G., & Goçer, F. (2018). Digital supply chain: A systematic review and future research directions. Computers in Industry, 101, 16-32.*

*https://doi.org/10.1016/j.compind.2018.04.017*

*Changes in Technical Education for Industry 4.0 - TEKLATAM (n.d.). TEKLATAM. https://teklatam.com/cambios-de-la-educacion-tecnica-con-miras-a-la-industria-4-0/*

*Chae, B. (2019). Supply chain management and the Industry 4.0: A review and research agenda. International Journal of Production Economics, 210, 1-13.*

*https://doi. org/10.1016/j. ijpe. 2019.01.007*

*Chae, B. (2019). Supply chain management and the Industry 4.0: A review and research agenda. International Journal of Production Economics, 210, 1-13.*

*https://doi. org/10.1016/j. ijpe. 2019.01.007*

*Choudhury, M., Paul, R., & Islam, M. S. (2019). Predictive analytics in supply chain management: A review. The International Journal of Logistics Management, 30(3), 785804. https://doi.org/10.1108/IJLM-05-2018-0131. https://doi.org/10.1108/IJLM-05-2018-0131*

*Copper Digital, Inc. (2023, May 4). The Future is Here: How Robotics is Driving Industry 4.0 Objectives. Copper Digital. https://copperdigital.com/blog/role-of-robotics-in-*

*achieving-industry-4-0-objectives/*

*Cristina (2021). Industry 4.0: the digital revolution in production processes. Geniotic Solutions. https://geniotic.es/industria-4-0/*

*Davenport, T. H. (2013). Analytics at work: Smarter decisions, better outcomes. Harvard Business Review Press.*

*Ejsmont, K., Gladysz, B., & Kluczek, A. (2020). Impact of Industry 4.0 on Sustainability-Bibliometric Literature Review. Sustainability, 12(14), 5650.*

*https://doi.org/10.3390/su12145650*

*Encyclopedia 1080 (n.d.). [Video]. https://www.encyclopedia.com/history/encyclopedias- almanacs-transcripts-and-maps/industrial-revolution-second.*

*Factory of the Future: How Industry 4.0 and AI Can Transform manufacturing (2023,*

*December 20). Bain. https://www. bain.com/insights/factory-of-the-future-how-industry-4-0-and-ai-can-transform-manufacturing/*

*Forces of change: Industry 4.0. Deloitte Insights.*

*https://www2. deloitte. com/us/en/insights/focus/industry-4-0/overview. html.*

*Future of industry 4.0. (n.d.). https://storm.genie.stanford.edu/article/future-of-industry-4.0- 262292*

*Garbie, I. H. (2017). Incorporating sustainability/sustainable development concepts in teaching industrial systems design courses. Procedia Manufacturing, 8, 417-423.*

*https://doi. org/10.1016/j.promfg. 2017.02.054.*

*Geissdoerfer, M., Savaget, P., Bocken, N. M. P., & Hultink, E. J. (2018). The circular economy - A new sustainability paradigm? Journal of Cleaner Production, 143, 757-768. https://doi. org/10.1016/j.jclepro. 2016.12.048*

*González, A., Arenas-Márquez, F. J., & Perales, F. J. (2020). Industry 4.0 and the impact on supply chain management: A literature review. IEEE Access, 8, 124633-124646. https://doi.org/10.1109/ACCESS.2020.3003442.*

*Hadnagy, C. (2018). Social engineering: The science of human hacking. Wiley.*

*Haseeb, M., Hussain, H. I., Slusarczyk, B., & Jermsittiparsert, K. (2019). Industry 4.0: A solution towards technology challenges of sustainable business performance. Social Sciences, 8(5), 154. https://doi.org/10.3390/socsci8050154.*

*Hashemi-Pour, C., Daniel, D., & Posey, B. (2024, May 16). Industry 4.0. Search ERP.*

*https://www.techtarget.com/searcherp/definition/Industry-40*

*Hazen, B. T., Boone, C. A., Ezell, J. D., & Jones-Farmer, L. A. (2014). Data quality for data science, predictive analytics, and big data in supply chain management: An introduction to the problem and suggestions for research and applications. International Journal of Production Economics, 154, 72-80. https://doi.org/10.1016/j.ijpe.2014.04.018.*

*Hazen, B. T., Boone, C. A., Ezell, J. D., & Jones-Farmer, L. A. (2014). Data quality for data science, predictive analytics, and big data in supply chain management: An introduction to the problem and suggestions for research and applications. International Journal of Production Economics, 154, 72-80. https://doi. org/10.1016/j. ijpe. 2014.04.018*

*Ibm (2024, 29 August). Industry 4.0. What is Industry 4.0? | IBM. https://www. ibm. com/topics/industry-4-0*

*Immerman, G. (2024, August 14). Emerging Industry 4.0 technologies with Real-World Examples. MachineMetrics. https://www. machinemetrics. com/blog/industry-4-0-.*

*technologies*

*Impact and benefits of Industry 4.0 in the supply chain. (n.d.). https://www. blog. metalinspec. com. mx/post/impacto-y-beneficios-de-la-industria-4-0- en-la-cadena-de-suministro.*

*India, P. (2021, September 2). Industry 4.0 and sustainable manufacturing - FutureBridge. FutureBridge.*

*https://www.futurebridge.com/industry/perspectives-mobility/industry-4- 0-and-sustainable-manufacturing/*

*Industry 4.0 and manufacturing ecosystems (n.d.). Deloitte Insights. https://www2.deloitte.com/us/en/insights/focus/industry-4-0/manufacturing-ecosystems- exploring-world-connected-enterprises.html.*

*Industry 4.0: Industrial Revolution in the heart of SDG Agenda 2030 | MIT Climate Portal (n.d.). MIT Climate Portal. https://climate.mit.edu/posts/industry-40-industrial-revolution- heart-sdg-agenda-2030.*

*Intelliarts (2024, May 15). Manufacturing 4.0: Explanation &Real-Worldexamples. Intelliarts. https://intelliarts.com/blog/manufacturing-4-0/*

*Jardine, A. K. S., Lin, D., & Banjevic, D. (2018). Predictive maintenance of industrial equipment.*

*Journal of Quality in Maintenance Engineering, 24(1), 2-17.*

*https://doi.org/10.1108/JQME-10-2016-0050*

*Kalsoom, T., Ahmed, S., Rafi-Ul-Shan, P. M., Azmat, M., Akhtar, P., Pervez, Z., Imran, M. A., & Ur-Rehman, M. (2021). Impact of IoT on Manufacturing Industry 4.0: A new triangular Systematic review. Sustainability, 13(22), 12506. https://doi.org/10.3390/su132212506.*

*Kamble, S. S., Gunasekaran, A., & Sharma, R. (2020). Industry 4.0 and its impact on supply chain management: A review and future research directions. International Journal of Production Research, 58(12), 3677-3700.*

*https://doi. org/10.1080/00207543.2020.1715092*

*Kamble, S. S., Gunasekaran, A., & Sharma, R. (2020). Industry 4.0 and its impact on supply chain management: A review and future research directions. International Journal of Production Research, 58(12), 3677-3700.*

*https://doi. org/10.1080/00207543.2020.1715092*

*Karimireddy, T., & Zhang, S. (2017). Incorporation of timing properties into adaptive error control methodfor timely and reliable communication in industrial automation networks.* Systems Science & Control Engineering, 5(1), 350-360.

*https://doi. org/10.1080/21642583.2017.1344945*

*Kaur, G., & Chauhan, P. (2024). Artificial Intelligence in Industry 4.0: Legal Analysis of Data Privacy Issues with Industry Stakeholders. In Apple Academic Press eBooks (pp. 187203). https://doi.org/10.1201/9781003414193-10*

*Kidwai, A. (n.d.). The Nine Pillars of Industry 4.0 - Technological Advancement. Polestarsolutions. https://www.polestarllp.com/blog/what-is-industry-40-and-its-nine- technology-pillars.*

*Kotter, J. P. (1996). Leading change. Harvard Business Review Press.*

*Kumar, A., Sarkar, B., & Parveen, M. (2020). The role of chatbots in improving customer experience. Journal of Business Research, 121, 252-263.*

*https://doi.org/10.1016/j.jbusres.2020.08.002*

*Kumar, S., & Singh, R. (2019). Internet of Things (IoT): A review on architecture, applications and challenges. International Journal of Computer Applications, 178(16), 1-5. https://doi.org/10.5120/ijca2019918614. https://doi.org/10.5120/ijca2019918614*

*Küpper, D., Lorenz, M., Knizek, C., Kuhlmann, K., Maue, A., Lassig, R., & Buchner, T. (2021, December 16). Advanced robotics in the factory of the future. BCG Global. https://www. bcg.com/publications/2019/advanced-robotics-factory-future.*

*Kurt, R. (2019). Industry 4.0 in terms of industrial relations and its impacts on labour life. Procedia Computer Science, 158, 590-601. https://doi.org/10.1016/j.procs.2019.09.093.*

*Kusiak, A. (2018). Smart manufacturing. International Journal of Production Research, 56(12), 1-10. https://doi.org/10.1080/00207543.2017.1393943.*

*Kusiak, A. (2018). Smart manufacturing. International Journal of Production Research, 56(12), 1-10. https://doi.org/10.1080/00207543.2017.1393943.*

*Lee, J., Bagheri, B., & Kao, H. A. (2014). A cyber-physical systems architecture for Industry 4.0- based manufacturing systems. Manufacturing Letters, 3, 18-23. https://doi.org/10.1016/j.mfglet.2014.12.001*

*Li, Q., Tang, W., & Li, Z. (2024). Leveraging Industry 4.0 for Sustainable Manufacturing: A Quantitative Analysis using FI-RST. Applied Sciences, 14(20), 9545. https://doi.org/10.3390/app14209545*

*Luce, R. (2020, February 10). Industry 4.0: Advanced technology creates new job opportunities. https://www.linkedin.com/pulse/industry-40-advanced-technology-creates-new-job- robert-luce.*

*Manufacturing Industry 4.0 Technologies | Microsoft Industry (n.d.).*

*https://www.microsoft.com/en-us/industry/manufacturing/resources/industry-4-0- technologies*

*Matana, G., Dal-Fabbro, I., & Gaviraghi, G. (2020). Method to assess the adherence of internal logistics equipment to the concept of CPS for industry 4.0. International Journal of Production Economics, 228, 107845. https://doi.org/10.1016/j.ijpe.2020.107845.*

*Mayer, C., & Oosthuizen, R. M. (2022). Sustainability in Industry 4.0 business practice: Insights from a multinational technology company. Frontiers in Sustainability, 3. https://doi. org/10.3389/frsus. 2022.886986*

*McKinsey & Company (2021). Cybersecurity in the age of digital transformation. McKinsey & Company.*

*MIT Technology Review (2024, April 11). Taking AI to the next level in manufacturing. MIT Technology Review. https://www. technologyreview. com/2024/04/09/09/1090880/taking-ai- to-the-next-level-in-manufacturing/*

*Owen-Hill, A. (n.d.). 10 Robotics Predictions for trends that will dominate 2023. https://blog. robotiq. com/10-robotics-predictions-for-trends-that-will-dominate-2023.*

*Porter, M. E., & Kramer, M. R. (2011). Creating shared value. Harvard Business Review, 89(12), 62-77.*

*Publishing, W. (2023, March 2). How AI serves as a cornerstone of Industry 4.0. Search Enterprise AI. https://www.techtarget.com/searchenterpriseai/feature/How-AI-serves- as-a-cornerstone-of-Industry-40.*

*Raut, R. D., Gardas, B. B., & Jha, M. K. (2020). Industry 4.0 technologies for sustainable development: A focus on energy efficiency and performance. Journal of Cleaner Production, 258, 120-134. https://doi.org/10.1016f.jclepro.2020.120134.*

*Raut, R. D., Gardas, B. B., & Jha, M. K. (2020). Industry 4.0 technologies for sustainable development: A focus on energy efficiency and performance. Journal of Cleaner Production, 258, 120-134. https://doi. org/10.1016/j.jclepro. 2020.120134*

*Rawat, G. S. (2024, June 4). Industry 4.0 explained: The 4th Industrial Revolution. Lio Blog. https://blog. lio. io/industry-4-0/*

*Rees, J. (2016). Industrialization and Urbanization in the United States, 1880 1929. Oxford Research Encyclopedia of American History.*

*https://doi. org/10.1093/acrefore/9780199329175.013.327*

*Ricadela, A. (2023, December 19). 10 Core components of Industry 4.0.*

*https://www.oracle.com/industrial-manufacturing/industry-4-components/*

*Ryalat, M., Franco, E., Elmoaqet, H., Almtireen, N., & Alrefai, G. (2024). The Integration of Advanced Mechatronic Systems into Industry 4.0 for Smart Manufacturing. Sustainability, 16(19), 8504. https://doi.org/10.3390/su16198504.*

*Shahriar, H., Islam, M. S., Jahin, M. A., Ridoy, I. A., Prottoy, R. R., Abid, A., & Mridha, M. F. (2024). Exploring Internet of Things adoption challenges in manufacturing firms: A Delphi Fuzzy Analytical Hierarchy Process approach. PLoS ONE, 19(11), e0311643. https://doi.org/10.1371/journal.pone. 0311643.*

*Simon (2023, December 30). 9 Smart Manufacturing Examples of Industry 4.0. Sustainability Success. https://sustainability-success.com/smart-manufacturing-examples-of-industry- 4-0/*

*Staff (2024, May 24). Industrial Revolutions: Summary, Causes, Consequences & Inventions - Historia Mundum. Historia Mundum. https://historiamundum.com/industrial- revolutions*

*Supply Chain 4.0 - the next-generation digital supply chain. (2016, October 27). McKinsey & Company. https://www. mckinsey. com/capabilities/operations/our-insights/supply-chain- 40--the-next-generation-digital-supply-chain.*

*Ta, T. (2024, October 17). IoT in manufacturing industry: applications, impacts and trends. Travancore Analytics. https://www. travancoreanalytics. com/iot-in-manufacturing-.*

*industry/*

*Talentedge (n.d.). Careers: Best jobs in the era of Industry 4.0 - Talentedge. https://talentedge.com/articles/careers-best-jobs-era-industry-4-0/*

*The Editors of Encyclopaedia Britannica (2024, October 5). Industrial Revolution | Definition, History, Dates, Summary, & Facts. Encyclopedia Britannica. https://www.britannica.com/event/Industrial-Revolution*

*The future of manufacturing: Industry 4.0 and job opportunities (n.d.). Hire Industrial. https://hireindustrial.com/blog/the-future-of-manufacturing-industry-4-0-and-job- opportunities*

*Thompson, G. (n.d.). Impact on society during the Industrial Revolution. worldhistory.org.uk. https://www. worldhistory. org. uk/industrial-revolution-impact-on-society.*

*UNESCO (2020). Education during COVID-19 and beyond. https://en. unesco. org/covid19/educationresponse.*

*Wadsworth, A., Mathers, K., & Gilliam, D. (2019). Development of IIoTmonitoring and control security scheme for cyber-physical systems. IEEE SoutheastCon 2019 Conference Proceedings, 1-5. https://doi.org/10.1109/SoutheastCon42311.2019.9020626. https://doi.org/10.1109/SoutheastCon42311.2019.9020626*

*Waller, M. A., & Fawcett, S. E. (2013). Data science, predictive analytics, and big data: A revolution that will transform supply chain design and management. Journal of Business Logistics, 34(2), 77-84. https://doi. org/10.1111/jbl. 12010.*

*Waller, M. A., & Fawcett, S. E. (2014). Data science, predictive analytics, and big data: A revolution that will transform supply chain design and management. Journal of Business Logistics, 35(2), 77-84. https://doi.org/10.1111/jbl.12010.*

*Waller, M. A., & Fawcett, S. E. (2014). Data science, predictive analytics, and big data: A revolution that will transform supply chain design and management. Journal of Business Logistics, 35(2), 77-84. https://doi. org/10.1111/jbl. 12010.*

*Wang, J., & Li, D. (2018). Adaptive computing optimization in software-defined network-based industrial internet of things with fog computing. Sensors, 18(8), 1351-1360. https://doi. org/10.3390/s18072139.*

*What are Industry 4.0, the Fourth Industrial Revolution, and 4IR? (2022, August 17). McKinsey & Company. https://www. mckinsey. com/featured-insights/mckinsey-explainers/what-are-industry-4-0-the-fourth-industrial-revolution-and-4ir.*

*Weflio - Digital Marketing Agency in León. (2022). Industry 4.0: What is it and how does it originate? Do you know it? Weflio.com. https://weflio.com/es/industria-4-0/*

*Wikipedia contributors (2024). Industrial Revolution. Wikipedia. https://en. wikipedia. org/wiki/Industrial_Revolution.*

*Wilde, R. (2019,). A Beginner's Guide to the Industrial Revolution. ThoughtCo. https://www.thoughtco.com/guide-to-the-industrial-revolution-1221914*

*Womack, J. P., & Jones, D. T. (2003). Lean thinking: Banish waste and create wealth in your corporation. Simon & Schuster.*

MIX
Papier aus verantwortungsvollen Quellen
Paper from responsible sources
FSC® C105338

Printed by Books on Demand GmbH, Norderstedt / Germany